Sea Animals

This book belongs to:

____

By Glorya Phillips

Oyster

Fish

Penguin

Starfish

Turtle

Sea Urchins

Sea Horse

Frog

Jellyfish

Lobster

Whale

Orca

Beluga

Dolphin

Shark

Stingrey

Manta ray

Octopus

Cuttlefish

Eel

Sail fish

Sawfish

Catfish

Thank you for choosing us.

We hope you enjoyed our book.

Your feedback is important to us, please let us
know how you like our book at:

 glorya.phillips@gmail.com

 www.facebook.com/glorya.phillips

 www.instagram.com/gloryaphillips